It hurts now, but I will look back on these moments & know God was molding me into something better: Someone more useful for His kingdom. That is the bigger picture, & I can't take my eyes off of it.

It hurts now, but not forever.

When I lighten my load, when I allow myself to breathe, I do better. When I stop trying to prove myself, I fail less. What's more, failing matters far less. We will all get where we need to be when we stop needing to get there. How ironic & frustrating. How freeing. I'm too busy tightening my corset to realize that my body looks more statuesque on its own. I can actually breathe without it, after all, God did not give it to me to put on. I look more comfortable, more natural. I must remember to breathe.

The fact that I don't feel God's presence with me should tell me He is closer than ever. Satan is smart, & he knows that if I feel far away I might actually start to believe it. God is right next to me, & I will not give in. I will not give Satan the satisfaction of making me think God has left me. I know too much scripture to believe it. I know my feelings shift & swell, but God is right here all the same. He's right here.

I don't notice how bad my fever is until the Holy Spirit's cool hand touches my forehead. I've got the Holy Spirit inside of me, I've got the medicine right here. When I start feeling the effects of sin in my life, when I pray & I feel like it's hitting the ceiling, I've forgotten that the very God I'm praying to has promised me so much more than forgiveness. I am given a shelter, I am offered healing. I get to constantly begin again.

David repeats himself many times in the Psalms. Some Psalms are almost word-for-word copies of each other. It's okay to sound like a broken record. It's okay to struggle with something for long stretches of time. In fact, the long fight is what God applauds. Don't give up, sanctification doesn't happen overnight. God works on a different timeline.

I love being raw with God. I love that we are brought to exhaustion, finally ready to give up, & only then do we feel the steady stream of water coming towards us. God knows exactly what He's doing. He works in the weak & in the soul that needs help. If the desert is the place I'm in, I have to remember that God is ready to pick me up when I fall. Falling, although it might hurt my pride, means I have finally grown tired of trying to do this without Him. The beautiful aftermath of the desert is surrender.

I cannot bury. I cannot hide. I have to bring it to You, even if it drags behind me. In Your light, everything burns. That is why Job says that after I am tested, I will come out like gold.

One of my favorite stories from the Bible is in Mark 9, when the man is begging Jesus to help him with his son who is possessed. Jesus is telling the man that anything is possible with belief. The father immediately says, "I believe, help my unbelief!" & I just love that. I know & believe so much about God, but when pressed I realize how much I doubt. The best part of it is that Jesus healed the man's son anyway. Jesus wanted transparency, not perfection. What a relief.

I love when a problem feels big & complex & I feel small & tired. My hands are numb because I'm writing in a journal all my little prayers, my eyes are welling up with water. I feel like I've run a marathon; the Holy Spirit has made that weight on my chest lift. I am still small & tired, but that problem has been handed off to a yoke that is easy, a burden that is light.

Breathe & say a little prayer. We are promised new mercies tomorrow, even if we feel like we've almost run out today.

I never expected God to fix the little things. They were so small I didn't even see them until now. The little bits of myself I had gotten used to being broken because the big issues were all I could see.

Yet, God sees fit to give me the joys of seeing every bit of me becoming more like Him. What an incredibly gracious Redeemer.

Ecclesiastes says that God has put eternity into man, & I really love that. It reminds me of 2 a.m. thoughts that feel big & hurt my chest. That need for more. The Holy Spirit fills that eternity-sized gap in me, & suddenly those haunting thoughts are so little. The ache in my chest goes away. I may be of small account, a vapor, like withering grass. But my God is all light, He is eternity. There is no reason to feel empty again.

I can't be enraged at other people's blindness. I can't be vengeful at other people who could be a victory of God's love someday. I will not stand in the way of their new testimony by ruining mine. God asks more of me, that I show compassion. My God demands that I understand.

The Bible says our hearts are desperately sick. It's okay not to understand everything I feel. It's okay to just pray & sleep on it, despite heavy emotions. God understands because Jesus walked through such nights too. Pass it on to the God whose burden is so, so light. The God who knows exactly how to heal.

I tell God these things until I believe them:

"I don't want a life You don't want for me."

"I will keep going until I see You."

"Break me again if You have to."

I think what we are taught as goodness & love is different than God's teaching of these things. His is a much less romanticized version. Once it begins to happen in our lives, what we pretend is love doesn't cut it anymore. It's difficult to understand that Job who lost everything, David who wrote some of the most pain-filled verses in the Bible, or the disciples who were all martyred had goodness & love follow them all the days of their lives. It doesn't look that way at times, but the Bible promises they did have goodness & love & that we do too. Maybe it isn't God who needs to fix our circumstances, maybe we need to change our perception of what goodness & love are.

What's wrong with slow moving? There is no need to be so impatient. Slow is good. It's better. It's okay for this journey to take time, little heart. It's building. Whatever it is.

Write out the lyrics to my favorite hymn, flip through my Bible & reread underlined sections, look through my journal at old entries. Getting back on track doesn't have to be done in one giant leap; God understands what a journey back home is. I don't take Him by surprise or upset Him by moving slowly. I can take my time, there is grace for me. He planned for me pulling away & needing to find my way back.

The Holy Ghost is constantly interceding on our behalf. The Bible says the Spirit groans to the Father when we struggle. When we don't know what to pray, the Holy Spirit is groaning for us, & the Father listens. Help is always coming in one form or another. God knows how helpless we are & makes provisions.

Sometimes I'm Martha in the kitchen. I'm frustrated & bitter. I'm angry. I'm comparing. I'm focused on details, wondering why Jesus & others are not. But I need to always be Mary. I must always be sitting at Jesus's feet. Listening. Listening. Listening. The details are not my job. Preparation is not the point. Jesus is always in my home. So, I must always be sitting with Him, ready to hear every word.

Rest is found in Christ. I must keep reaching for that book. I must keep moving. I want it to be in everything else, but it is in just one place.

There will be times when there is nothing else I can do but know that God loves me. & you know, those times are good too. Then one day, the way out of that hole is clear, & I keep moving. Being "stuck" is not all bad; I can still work for His glory. & what a gift in & of itself that is.

It becomes an idol to me to understand it all. I have to keep reminding myself that no one has ever completely grasped what God was doing through them. A perfect answer to my problems is not in specifics. It doesn't even need to make sense to me for God to work. It is not of me. I only have to be present & willing.

There is no sin, secret or revealed, that should keep us from talking to God & from asking His hand to be on our lives. Sin does not mean you are shut out or silenced forever. Repenting & moving forward makes the "mountain melt like wax," "rough way made smooth," "crooked road made straight," & "valley filled." The Lord will honor it. Pray & see.

I do not need to sit down to pray & have everything figured out by the end. God is about process. It's not that He can't get through to me, it is that sitting with Him is the most important thing. I need to be willing to sit & have nothing else that could matter more. That's how I begin.

You will preserve me. You always have & always will. You will preserve me. That is what You are in the business of doing. Even when it feels differently. That's what God is doing all the time. Keeping me close to Him. Keeping me. Until we are face to face.

Please remember that God is about process, little heart. I'm saying it to you again, that I don't have to figure out sin all at once, only work on what God is pressing on. I am important & loved. He loves me. He does not hate me. I am not bad because I have things to work on. God does not want self-loathing. God is hopeful for me because He is working on me. All of these things are full of goodness & love.

What a humbling thought, that Jesus has more for me.

My own insecurities make me feel like I need to be everything. I know I did not receive that from the Lord because He knows I don't have to be everything.

Being everything is not our job, it's His. God carries that responsibility perfectly because that's who He is. Letting go & giving things up to Him is what we are made for.

No matter what my anxieties, depressions, or bad thought processes tell me, God is leading me where I need to go. When I cling to gospel, I get to let go of so much that weighs on my heart, & that's so relieving despite any trial. A life walking with Jesus is a life learning freedom.

I was made for a purpose. Spread the love that Jesus has given me. There is so much room to figure out what God wants me to do with my specific gifts. That isn't supposed to be anxiety-producing; there is a certain liberty, a creativity to it. It's okay to not understand everything. We're not supposed to. There is freedom in constantly giving Him our worries about this. Just love & pray & have patience. We can do it. God knows we can.

I am learning so slowly that blessings are not earned in any
conventional sense, & they are not always given. Moses didn't
go to the promised land. Job lost everything he could have
loved. Jeremiah felt betrayed by how he was treated by the
people he witnessed to, by the God he was witnessing for.
They continued to work out their salvation with fear &
trembling. It's still possible, even if I don't get what I thought
I needed.

The Bible refers to our "inward being" multiple times. It is also called our "secret heart." I just find it so comforting to know that what we are dealing with emotionally & mentally is known. When I am struggling with something that feels big inside of me, I then remember Jesus struggled too. That it's okay.

I just find it so comforting that Jesus had anxiety & stress & emotion & sleep deprivation & a physical reaction to all of that in one breakdown. It's recorded in the Bible. We are not alone. We have a God who understands human pains, every single one of them. Let me never forget what company I am keeping when I am weakened.

I always appreciate the gift of going through a really difficult season & coming out of it humbled & more empathetic. Sometimes that's the only gift to be recognized at the time, & that's okay. It's okay if I don't get why it happened, if I never understand why. So long as I become fruitful in ways I may never have expected.

I know You. I know You do not abandon. These waves will not drown me. You have found me. You never lost me.

Do you talk back to the enemy? Do you tell that voice in your head that says depression is your natural state that it's a lie? Do you tell that voice that you aren't just treading water, that instead you are growing? That panic attacks aren't everything there is to experience? Talk back to it, tell it to get out. Tell it that trying is the point, getting back up is the point. Keep going, little heart, this is not over. You are not permanently fixed in this spot.

It's okay to think about your smallness. It's okay that you got a little lost. He leaves the 99 to come find you. To find me. That's good, good news. Smallness is okay because God is so big & cares so much for us.

Doubt & insecurity are things God does not give me. Reducing myself to the same pattern of wallowing, double checking, sitting statically, praying again, doubting… God did not give me that pattern. Becoming confident in how Jesus is working in my life starts with moving forward & decreasing myself.

Jesus felt weak & tired, He got frustrated, He wept aloud, He grieved, He sweat blood from great stress & anxiety, He felt physical pain. This is who I am praying to. The One who knows.

I think that sometimes we forget that God does not merely tolerate us. David said some very transparent things to God, & He was still listening. God cared a great deal about David's thoughts, worries, joys, etc. no matter what David was going through or had done.

We are not slaves. We are each considered a temple, a beloved, a child. How humbling.

I must always remember, always, that no matter what I believe I deserve…Christ believes I deserve Him. He created me for this. Grace is something He created for me to have. I can, my little heart can. I can take grace for myself, I can believe in myself. He believes in my abilities because He gave them to me.

I think it's important that the phrase "but as for me" is used in the Bible so much. There are so many instances where people had to reevaluate their loyalty to other things/people vs. their loyalty to the Lord. It was personal to them because the gospel is personal. My relationship with the gospel is up to me.

One of the bigger lies I had to free myself of is that being kind is the most important goal. It was there, & I never questioned it. I ended up unhealthy, depressed, bitter, & incredibly anxious about how I was getting run over by my own life. So, I am actively striving for something else now. Being kind happens naturally (as do many other good qualities) when the most important goal is loving Jesus & whom He made me to be. That is more than kind, it's everything.

You know something? I am coming out of a season feeling exactly like that. Really bitter & confused & angry about everything. But I was back reading Job after church because my teacher asked us about seeing other people's needs. This is what I said:

I think you can see other people's needs better after you can declare your own. I think we all chase this idea of feeling good when the best feeling is being able to declare where you really are. Job does that, chapter after chapter of his feelings & his anger & his pain, & he gets it all out. Then God finally speaks, & Job is able to be humbled & silent. We all want to do the second part, but the first part is how we get there. In doing that, you can finally get your eyes off of yourself. You can see others more clearly; you can see yourself more clearly & God himself. The Lord works through your obedience, your repentance, your emotions, so long as they are your true ones.

Job 38 is one of my all-time favorite chapters of the Bible. It seems counterintuitive for the Lord to be talking about himself to Job who is in a lot of pain. If we did that, it would be very insensitive. But the Lord knows how to lift our eyes. The Lord is always right. He is. Where was I when He laid the foundation of the earth? I wasn't in existence yet, He hadn't created me yet. But He did. It's for reasons like this.

Fruitfulness starts with honesty, & I am grateful.

Go talk to Him, little heart. Tell Him everything. He can take it & do something with it that we could never do. He can heal it.

I can't stop thinking about Elijah sitting underneath the juniper tree & asking God to die. God sent an angel who said, "This journey is too much for you" & that he must eat. Elijah did, then he rested. He woke still feeling hopeless, & the angel repeated himself.

It took Elijah longer than he wanted to get better. Sometimes we want to move, but we can't. Sometimes the journey is too much. It is not a sin to understand limitations. Start there, get stronger, then get up.

There is only one truth. There is only one thing we can safely cling to. The gospel of Christ not only refuses to or doesn't want to, but it cannot fail me. It is an okay thing to let myself take it. Christ died so I could. Isn't that wonderful? How safe it is to accept the gospel into my life.

It is becoming more & more clear to me that our plans are fleeting & unreliable. That guarding our hearts is the best way, that God's way is the best way. I don't know much else except that I want to be the best helper to Your cause, & I've got feelings pulling me in many directions, but I will wait for You to tell me what to do, & I will work on wanting & doing just that.

In an attempt to curb a panic attack, this is what I wrote:

God does not want me to fear so much that I cannot move. God does not want me to fear the world at all. There is no guilt involved in loving the Jesus who died for me. He did not give me a spirit of slavery, only one of freedom.

I think the reason the Bible insists that shame is not meant to be felt by Christians is because it keeps us from really pressing into the Lord, which is the most important thing we can do in our entire lives. It keeps us so far away from not just the benefits of grace, like joy or gratitude, but grace itself. It keeps us from hearing "It is finished" in our daily lives, & Jesus died just to give us that, to help us understand how much love there is, how well it fights against sin & the pain it causes.

Distance from Christ is only because we push Him out, not because He ever desires it. Closeness with Christ is our medicine, & it is okay to access it. I am not just allowed; He desires to talk with me with all He is.

Heaven felt closer to me today than it has in a long
time. Maybe because I felt more planted on Earth. More
rooted in myself. It makes me want Heaven that much more.
It makes me want to praise God for all He has done, even if I
don't understand it all, because one day I will speak to Him
with no barrier & no burdens. What an amazing thing not
only to feel today, but to always know is coming.

The Bible has imagery of putting on the things of God as armor to protect myself. A shield of faith. A breastplate of righteousness. Shoes of readiness…

If I am afraid, I have the defense. If I am lonely, I have the defense. If I am exhausted, I have the defense. If I am struggling with a certain sin, I have the defense. If I am weakened, I have the defense.

It's okay to put on the armor of God. It's okay to ask God for what I need. He is a ready & willing participant in this relationship. I can talk to God about what I need, & through grace, He will give it to me. I am not alone.

Sometimes I don't read my Bible because I am afraid of the words on its pages. I'm afraid of what I won't understand, what I will recoil from. The fear in me is of myself & that the Lord will not approve of my lack of belief. If my enjoyment of Him is not automatic, is it even authentic? God says it is. The only reason I am trying to be close is made of Him too. His goodness & His light. He is always willing when I want to open the door for Him. He stands at the door & knocks, wanting to sit in my home with me, to be near.

Every verse is there for me, even if I flinch or can't understand it in the beginning. Every prayer to Him is heard. I don't have to have my eyes on myself, it's okay to look at Him. He understands me. He knows me better than I know myself. If I believe that, it is the beginning of understanding Him.

Hearts can feel very heavy, & it's hard to fight against that current. The pull to dive into pains can be strong. It feels like I won't be myself unless I hold on to things that I needed at one time.

I can look up tomorrow, though. That is okay. Giving myself permission to see other things is the kind of warm that belongs in my heart, it doesn't always have to burn from an ache.

I am moving slowly these days, trying to only bring what is good with me. I take tearful & scared steps forward. I'm not sure where I'm going, but God is. He is teaching me so many things.

Bad things have happened. Bad things will continue to happen. I am not as scared as I once was. I have learned, I have become something else that can take in more. I have cleaned out my heart, I had to force myself. Yet…I have room for all this light.

Shifts & swells scare us; we jump at them. We point, always feeling small, sometimes feeling angry, *How we will we survive this?*

Little heart, survival is not the point.

Little heart, God is with us.

"Long-suffering" is not referring to me forcing myself to stay with manipulative/toxic people.

"Loving-kindness" is not a trait that should allow people to take advantage of me.

"Quiet & gentle spirit" does not mean that I ignore warning signs/red-flags.

Being a Christian does not mean I lack standards in personal life. It means the opposite. Jesus died for me. That is how much I am worth to Him. I will take care of myself.

Little pieces of me. They are hidden. They get lost. What a good thing then that God is on record since the very beginning calling our names when we hide.

I keep thinking I need to see God in every situation, but I just need to trust that He was there.

He was. He is.

When a time of year like this comes up & I see how really wary I am of so much, it is hard to feel like God is seeing what I'm seeing in myself. Even outside of me, everything is too close, too claustrophobic, too material. My eyes only see what is in front of me, which is a zoom-in on my faults & worries & past. Maybe it's because the idea of happiness & this kind of artificial joy is what surrounds certain seasons. It can be really painful.

They say, my heart says, "This is how you're supposed to feel."

God says, "I see how you feel. I have felt how you feel. This doesn't last forever."

Today I was thinking about the angry brother in the prodigal son parable. How his sense of self matched his brother's before he left. The father was always willing to talk through any pain, insecurity, or anger, but both of his sons didn't understand. One physically left their home, & the other mentally left. We hardly ever understand either. That's okay, there is so much grace for it all.

It's okay to stay home. It's okay to come back if I left. I may be away now, but I can come back.

For the first time in a very long time, I felt the grace of the Lord in my thoughts about myself. God forgets my sin, He creates a gap in between me & my past so wide it is infinite. It's Jesus. I ask & always receive.

One of the most important messages of the Bible I have ever grasped is that God mourns for & with me. I struggle with not feeling guilty. I struggle with blaming myself in a way that does not help but hinders.

The Lord mourns for me. It makes me cry just thinking about it. The Lord mourns with me when my heart hurts. There is no room for guilt there. Only acceptance of pain & waiting for Him to move.

& He will.

Sometimes it's just zooming out from my little life & seeing the scope of what God has done to protect & help that makes me see Him clearly, & then myself. Those thoughts that feel truthful about me are just fears. I am fearing the wrong thing. Those thoughts aren't true because He won't allow that to be the end for me. Because I will ask God for hope in His love & for deliverance to be kept alive in whatever famine comes.

This isn't about me & my sin. Jesus took care of me & my sin on the cross, & I am not alone in any fight I ask God to be a part of.

God does instantaneous miracles before the crossing of the Red Sea…but with this work, He "drove the sea back by a strong east wind all night & made the sea dry land, & the waters were divided."

God works in His timing. Sometimes His works are in the dark, sometimes it takes all night.

I have what feels like a little stone in my chest, & it makes me angry. I keep telling God that I want a renewed heart that has better things to give Him. He keeps saying all I need to do is love the one He gave me.

Nothing is easy, & everything is.

When I begin to believe in my control over events, I also begin to fear, to stack up odds, to press, to get too involved, to become so much more pained. There is something good about letting go, not just because of blessings or protection from all of that, but because I don't have to fight so much of my life. God does that for me. It gives me so much room. He gives me so much room to breathe.

I always have to work these facts like a muscle.

I will make so many more mistakes in this life. God knows
about them all. He sent Jesus, who taught us then bled &
sacrificed Himself for us all. That's where my sins end in His
eyes, in His power to move beyond all human capabilities. It's
the rising from the dead. All those mistakes are known
factors that God has taken care of. Forgiveness for each
other, for myself; it all starts & ends there. Gratefulness &
joy. Steadfastness & gaining freedom. Moving beyond pain.
Moving beyond it all.

I have to work at making the story of Jesus strong in my
mind's eye.
It is okay that it is not easy; Jesus's life wasn't easy either.
I have to keep thinking about Him, about this. It's where
everything is to me. He's everything.

I was feeling scared & foggy again for a few days. All hollow
& upset. But today I woke up with a clear mind & calm heart.

Sometimes things are not fruition, & that is a good thing.
Heavy days are not always here.

Getting frustrated at people who do not know Christ comes naturally to me. Impatience or meanness or caving in from what's said or done. Yet their sanctification process hasn't even started. They don't know the Holy Spirit, they have never met God in a way that has permeated throughout their life.

Talk to the Holy Spirit about walking with people, about how hard it is. It is hard. Yet in my own life, most fruit in those relationships doesn't come through one conversation. It comes through withstanding all of their defenses that were created long before you got there & showing them what Christ has done. Take time to prepare what to say, how to say it. You can do this.

As of late, I have been very humbled by how sharp my tongue can be, how much my heart doesn't understand others. I hate thinking like that, like I can't stretch my heart around something enough to get to it. It's this moment when I know I just have to say, "Explain this more. I'd really like to know" & listen more, stretch more than I knew I could. I may have a new heart, a new mind, but it takes getting used to. God knew it would.

God will use this for good. Do not be afraid to believe it now before you can see it, little heart. It is what you are made for—to trust Him.

I cried over something important just now. It was good for me. It was a pain that moved from my chest to my cheeks & out of me. Right out of me. It came out just to weigh over my hands. It will come back, more than likely, but I thought it was going to stay here in my chest. I'm so glad it reached my eyes. I am grateful to God for pain. I don't know how that can be.

Love by its nature is not passive. It extends to everyone. God by nature is not passive. God extends to everyone. I don't get to pick who receives it from me while continuing to consider myself aligned with Christ's message.

Something that has helped me recently is thinking of that verse in Isaiah which says, "Who are you that you are afraid of man who dies?" every time I'm anxious. It makes me think of my fear as an extension of pride. I don't have any reason to be afraid when I zoom out of it in that way. I don't know, I think of it every time I start fidgeting, & it's been really good for me.

You have days set apart for me. You have moments made for me that will have me in trial, in desert, in upset. You have time created for me to laugh & have love & to be breathless. I cannot wait for any of it. I am so excited to see what You want for me. Trials will make me stronger & more humble for You. All of these moments will make me sing to You. I don't want to miss a second of God's glory.

I used so much of myself when I thought I needed to make a way to access the joy of the Lord in order to receive it. The Lord gives it, though. It is not of me. When I set all things down, there is room in my hands to be handed the light-filled things.

I belong where God believes I should be, & it's so close to Him.

God is in control for good, good reasons. I wish I didn't rebel against that so much. He understands. He knows. It's okay that I don't.

My God heard every prayer & knew better than to give my wants to me.

Pain molds. Pain teaches. Pain lessens.

Joy of the Lord fills in the gaps.

I am always learning how to forgive, how to be better, how to be less hard on myself. I will never reach the top of this mountain, but I must never stop climbing it.

Jesus wasn't doing anything but enduring on the cross, but He was doing so much. I can be alone & doing good. I can be in pain & doing good. I can be setting up others for health as I process something hard for me. He is the example set for my every moment.

I keep telling God that I just can't see what I'm supposed to do next. I'm trying to look at that as a good thing. Here is where I just sit with God because of who He is, not to get an answer.

I think when we get angry about sins we commit, we get even more impatient with others when they don't. Why are they not as self-loathing as we are? Do we not deserve some credit for all of our pains to hate ourselves for what we've done?

Except God doesn't want you to collapse in on yourself. He doesn't hate you. He hates only what you do to yourself because He loves *you*.

You can do this. He believes in you. It's okay to lift your eyes, little heart. We are not alone in anything.

This season is a long one, but I have this feeling of being rooted deeper in the ground. I'm stretching & becoming.

God does not want me to hurt by giving people trust who are known to be toxic or lack wisdom. I should forgive them, absolutely, but also stand my ground. I must be so careful with myself. If Jesus left those who didn't want to hear Him, I can too.

Tears that appear without force. A song you've listened to so much that it sounds like the laugh of an old friend. A growing sunflower. A coming up for air. Trying to reach the light. This season is a healing cut. It's such a strain.

-

Months after writing this, I can say Satan cannot bully you forever. He cannot pain you without reproof.

Some seasons rip roots out & churn soil, but those sunflowers I talked about…they grew. I didn't know they would.

I kept telling God, *I don't know what to do. I'm so upset. Please show me what I'm supposed to do.* & I am so surprised at what God has been wanting from me:

process,

feel less guilt for that.

God does not want me to run away from Him. He knows exactly who I am & loves me very much. I do not need to feel shame to make God finally approve of me. I need to step into grace, not a kind of self-punishment.

God is confident in His decision to love.

& love well.

Faith is unseen & sometimes not felt. It is in our actions. I intend to see things through, whatever those things end up being. He picked me, & I will always be trying to pick Him back.

My body can feel when a situation lacks health. Listen. I am not being dramatic. This isn't a non-issue. I am worth getting better, & I am worth making a decision.

Practice it until I believe it, then celebrate. God is something to celebrate.

Chest is heavy? Keep breathing. Breathing isn't steady? Lean back. Limbs are rigid? Let them relax. Shoulders rising? See if they will drop just a little bit.

One thing at a time, small adjustments, little victories. Because moving slowly is okay. It's good. Most of the time, it actually gets us where we need to go.

I don't know God's will for me, & He gives little insight for a reason. I must continue to cling & pursue even if that dream goes up in smoke. That's painful for me to type or even think about, but if God's will is different, who am I to think I had it all figured out the right way?

That's the thing about spiritual mistakes. You always come back stronger, better, more prepared next time. I want God, not my angle on an over-simplified version of Him. If I really ask for Him, that's what I'll get, & in doing so it will reveal my shortcomings.

Jesus looks right at us, & He sees us. It is the most humbling, heartbreaking, healing thought I know of. He forgives me & paid for my lack of forgiveness towards others on the cross. My priority is that. My love is with that. My life is trying to be like Him. Very imperfectly, but there is grace for me & you as we learn to forgive & love ourselves & so many other things.

You get to allow yourself to let it go. You get to talk to God about pain & anger. He can take it. He can. I promise because He promises. Releasing it releases you from them. God believes you deserve that, & so do I.

The cross already outed you as a person with a sick heart in the same way it outed us all. The debt has already been paid for our sins, our badness. Jesus knows exactly who you are, which is why He died for you. In this same way, Jesus knows exactly who I am, which is why He died for me. To be with us forever because He loves us.

We can learn a lot about how to love someone else with that as our example. There is so much still to learn about how to love ourselves.

Self-loathing feels like protecting myself, but it isn't.

Hiding feels like guarding myself, but it isn't.

Second-guessing myself feels like wisdom, but it isn't.

There is a way to engage with doubt that doesn't feed it, but shrinking away isn't it.

I think somewhere along the line I got the idea that everything either makes me a good or bad person. It's easy to do as a Christian especially. I keep trying to make everything in my life worth something to God…when there is just no need to put that pressure on my heart. I heard the phrase "morally neutral" the other day, & it has helped me so much. Some things are just there.

I don't need to feel guilty for being careful. Jesus was so careful with His time here & with us.

Pressure on my heart does not make pain go away, I think I always knew that. Sometimes I wanted it to stay because I thought it felt better than the idea of letting the pressure go. I thought the weight would turn me into something else. But dropping it does more, it's given me room to breathe. I now have room to look up. That's more satisfying than anything I have ever held close to me.

I think a lot of times I find myself trying to be a driving force in someone. I don't think that's fair for me or them. I can't sustain being that way, & they can't sustain weight I'm putting on their heart. We are meant to encourage & empower, to love, but we are not meant to be everything. We are meant to be human.

Being salt & light means that they will see my example through behavior & encouraging words & not have it forced on them through anger or ultimatums before they are let into the Christian community. No one holds the key to being a part of this family, & no one decides what is in someone's heart except for God.

It is okay that wonderful & light things come in waves, just like it is a relief that disappointing & heavy things don't last forever. To everything there is a moment, a day, a whole season. Enjoying or hurting, each moment has a purpose. A purpose that isn't mine.

On the first page of the book of Job in my Bible, I wrote, "The book of 37 chapters of silence" because God did not say one word to Job until chapter 38, though Job wanted answers & help long before that. I know the feeling.

Jesus came to Earth to die for & save us. There is peace in this fact that surpasses all confusion. Job in chapter 19 says, "For I know my Redeemer lives & at last He will stand upon the earth."

& at last…Jesus did. The same God will show up for you. He always does & always has. In the silence, it is important to remember who stood upon the earth for us.

We are more than mental problems. Joy is coming. I still believe it. I'm moving towards it all the time. He gives us our food in due season, He really does.

God will work on me so that I will ultimately be used for His purpose. Even in my failures. I don't know if I can thank Him enough for that.

I think that dry spells should be normalized. They are a part of everyone. I am in one myself. We are inconsistent & little; God isn't. I am no less loved when I feel "lukewarm" than when I feel close to Christ. When I get anxious in the way of guilt for lack of feeling towards God, I remember that God's presence in my life does not come from guilty feelings or making myself do something, it comes from Christ & the sacrifice He made. It is not anxiety that saves us, & it is not our home. Jesus is. That is the thing to celebrate & move forward on whether it feels like it in my little heart or not.

Take the time to see how you are feeling. I have gotten myself in a very bad place because I just got used to destructive thoughts & the following emotions. Please, remember that good days are supposed to happen to you, too.

I think sometimes healing sounds like a bad process because some wounds are old. It's okay for them to heal. It's okay to have those things be in the past. I am not letting go of anything good, I am letting go of things I have grown accustomed to having.

Oh, what is God going to do with my frantic little heart? What will He do with it being bent toward the serious & anxious? Where is the joy I know I am to be a part of as His child? I struggle to find what is all around me. Look up, little heart. It is there. It is meant for me.

I think preparing for the worst may not be doing You justice. Trying to plan an escape route for what I'm praying for… *What will I do when I'm not enough? What will I do when it doesn't get answered?* These aren't fair. Doubting myself is doubting the God who knows what He's doing.

We are so fortunate to have a God who doesn't treat us like we owe Him. He doesn't want us to live like we are under His thumb. He wants love & celebration instead.

God not answering a prayer of mine; Him creating a different plan for me does not mean that this one was a failure. God moving me to another plan is just the reality—the lot God gave me for my good & His Glory. That's it. It's not about me. It's all Him. For Him. It makes me grateful to be a part of it at all.

So I will move forward now.

But God will get you there. God will help you.

I must not look to other people's sin as the reason why the cross is necessary. That's how much my sin means to Jesus. It didn't take other people's failures for the world to hate Him. Jesus would have been sweating "great drops of blood" in the garden if I was the only sinful person to ever be on the planet. That's how much He cares for me. Him being "pierced for our transgressions & crushed for our iniquities" is on me. Jesus "tasting death for everyone" is for me. My sin. My shortcomings. My failures. I must not let pride take away my understanding that Jesus sacrificed for me.

These haunted things will have light on them eventually.

Our God is one of new beginnings. Start over. Start over every day. Remember how many chances He has given in the past.

The difficult & the slow-moving things eventually, eventually bear more fruit than anything. Do not give up. Do not stop praying. God will keep you moving forward. It's the only good way. The only way we can grow, & we will.

I am glad God is so patient. I am so slow to learn. I'm glad He calls me His clay, His child, His temple to stay in. What an identity to rest in. God is patient because my identity is His plan.

God is not in the business of terror or anxiety, & what a comforting thought in the midst of such things.

God honors what you are doing for Him now.

It's impressive to me just how often David & others say "be not far from me," "incline Your ear to me," "hear my prayer," or even "O Lord, I call upon You."

So much asking to be received. There is so much humility in those words, I wonder who I would be if I asked to just be heard by the Lord before I spoke to Him. How sure I would want to be of my words to others, or myself, if I started with the Lord first.

You will get there in the same way we all do, stumbling & failing & getting back up & looking up at who made it all possible. You will be blessed because of who God is, not who you are.

The cross decided what you were worth everything. The same goes for others in your life who will need to understand grace & the Lord well to love you well. The Lord decided a long time ago that is something we all deserve.

One of the hardest facts I have ever faced is that some are enemies of me, enemies of my Lord. David seems to be so factual about this, often repeating to have the Lord destroy them. I have always had a hard time understanding that.

-

I think God answers that plea a very few times. He hears what He already knew, that some do not trust Him, that most do not believe in Him.

When I read verses like "In your book were written, every one of them, the days that were formed for me, when as yet there was none of them," I think of the mundane & unmanageable parts of my day first. *Did God plan it? Did God mean for me to feel so rotted?*

The Holy Spirit immediately presses on my heart for thinking so. He knows why I have felt so rotted; it is because I refused to be looking at God in those moments.

I hyper-focus on myself, then blame Him for not agreeing with me when I see the faults I created. Of course, He believes in better for me than a lack of joy in Him. He is the one who wants joy for me more than I ever could.

Trust, trust, trust. It is the only way out of rumination.

Renaissance is the word for when I look at myself in the mirror now. It feels like a renewal of health & of care. All things new. How I would imagine the prodigal son looked at his home when he believed he would return to it, begging to be allowed to serve there. It's the same home, but it is no longer a cage. *I'll serve in whatever way I can. How can I help?*

I cry imagining what the Lord would say about that. Of me finally taking care of the body He gave me. Of the person He loves. Taking care of myself is loving Him.

I like that I can leave looking at myself after that.

During a dry season I inevitably get to a space in which I keep trying to see Him, feel Him, hear from Him. *Time to separate all my bad from His good. I was taught this. What are You trying to tell me? What is this that I can't see?* It's what I ask Him over & over.

Why was I always so angry about it? It took me a long time to realize I was asking myself that question. It wasn't for God to answer.

God is in me. He is already in me. He's here. He gives. I don't have to take. I have no ability to yank anything away from Him anyway, there is no need to be so volatile. I was yanking at me. I was criticizing me. I always end up in this desert only to shove God away so I could be alone.

As Gomer pushed her husband away, He only loved her more.

It's time to go Home. Now.

I just now came to an understanding. I can take idols out of my life even if I moved them in. Paul says it. God says it. I can leave it behind now. There is no shame in Christ. There is no shame in the cross. Jesus died willingly so I could pick up the idols I put in my temple, my little heart, & move them where they belong. I am religious in every way, that's how God made me. How God made you. It's okay to believe it now even if we didn't before.

Christ is knocking, so He will help me move idols out. They're heavy, they're stone, it makes me hot & scared to move them out by myself. He can help you move them out. He can bring people in your life to help you.

I'm already too angry. I'm too angry to be writing to You. I have nothing but shaking, deep breaths to offer. It's as if there is a blurry film on Your word as I flip these pages.

Is this what You meant? I ask it, terrified. *Is this what Jesus meant when He said only a few will understand?*

I see in Joshua now, after he falls on his face in front of You, he asks You, "& what will You do for Your great name?"

You are frustrated back, You say, "Get up! Why have you fallen on Your face?"

It's a bit clearer to me now that what You do for Your great name is You let us finish believing we aren't good enough, You sit with us & listen. You listen & listen as You are taking our anger away, & You hold a mirror up. You almost always ask questions back at us. How we must look as we try to judge You. How silly it is to blame You or believe we cannot see Your words. I can if I look at them.

I can.

There is no chance in my life with God. There is nothing He does not put here, not my humor or pain. It is a hard thing to make peace with; everything in my life is His because my life is His.

It is the fear of not understanding that makes us stay in lack of knowledge. It is the fear of looking ignorant & not the ignorance itself. When it says, "This saying was hidden from them, & they did not grasp what was said," it is because they did not talk to each other. They did not find someone who did understand. They did not follow Jesus & beg for understanding as others did. They just left Him.

Jump in, little heart. He is not afraid of my ignorance of Him, only of my lack of repentance. We are little, He is not. It is the point of it all.

I did not praise & I did not praise for a long time. I was incredibly broken.

But I am glad that I knew He was God while I was silent, even more while I cried out. I am glad He gave me that knowing. I will sing soon. I know that too.

I talk to God at night until it feels less like I'm rubbing
against a bruise & more like I'm drinking cool water.

God does not want me to run away from Him. He knows exactly who I am & loves me very much. I do not need to feel shame to make God finally approve of me. I need to step into grace, not self-punishment.

I am always surprised, although I shouldn't be, that there are so many things in my Christian life I have to relearn, look over again, & pray about more. Pride is so a part of me that there are times I think God allows me to forget the lesson I learned last season, so I can be humbled by how much help I always need.

I wish people talked about how to search for God while struggling with mental health more. Sometimes I don't feel Him at all. Sometimes I don't feel like myself, so much so that I can't find my way back to whatever I was before. Sometimes nothing in my life or in myself makes any sense to me. Sometimes I am completely overwhelmed by my circumstance. In this season, my thoughts, emotions, body, & spiritual strength are collapsing in on themselves.

But hear me.

I am not doing anything wrong because this is happening to me. My weakness is not an evil, hated, or wasted trait. It's okay to talk to God about all of the above if you are having this happen too. God never wants forced functionality. He asks for you to hold tight. This isn't over for me or you. Jesus had breakdowns too. The cross wasn't the ending for any of us, including Jesus himself. I imagine it felt differently to Him in the moment; I know it does for me.

A resurrection happened anyway. I am now praying for one of my own.

"If these were silent, the very stones would cry out" is so humbling to me. If not me, there is someone, even something else to praise Him. I might as well lift my voice. I might as well try. He wants me to, He knows I can. He believes I can praise Him.

Oh, Immanuel. God is with us. It is the greatest gift.

The disillusionment of my praising the Lord came out of disillusionment of others.

Others are not intercessors for Jesus. Jesus is the intercessor. Jesus is God. This is only God & I. I do not have to go through them to believe in Him.

"For with the Lord there is steadfast love, & with Him is plentiful redemption."

It seems like God knew I would need to exhale. Steadfast, plentiful. There is so much of His goodness that I don't need to worry. This is just one sentence written over Him. This is just one comfort of a book that has a life of its own. The comfort never ends. The fears will all drown in waves God can calm for me.

Doubt leads to exhaustion. I am exhausted all the time. It's as if all my monsters are in on my desire to make them leave. *Get out. Get away. I am too tired for this.*

"Then believe," He tells me.

I only want to say okay to You because I know I'm supposed to. My eyes well up as I think over the fact.
Then why am I crying?

It is because I believe, but I don't know how.

Little heart, believing is going to sleep. Believing is trusting.

"Beware of false prophets, who come to you in sheep's clothing but inwardly are ravenous wolves. You will recognize them by their fruits. Are grapes gathered from thorn bushes, or figs from thistles? So every healthy tree bears good fruit, but the diseased tree bears bad fruit."

I have missed the fact that bad fruit can still be there. It isn't that disingenuous people bear no fruit at all, or that evil is clearly marked by complete lack of. It is that from far away it will still look like good fruit if I assume it must be there. From a distance it might seem worth coming closer. When I do get close, I cannot confirm my bias that everyone will have the good I imagine. I only imagine to make myself *feel* safe. If I see fruit that looks good but has bruises inside, worms inside, disease underneath it's skin, I have to leave to *be* safe.

I thought I could sense disingenuous people by their lack of fruit completely or by the amount of health that surrounds them. That is not what the verse says though. It is the kind of fruit. It is looking at for what is. What kind of fruit is when I look at it? Is it love, joy, peace, patience, kindness, goodness, faithfulness, gentleness, self-control?

I don't have to carry around haunted things in order to feel at home. Once I realize I'm not where I need to be, that I'm not thinking on what I need to be thinking about, there is now a question that comes to mind.

"Do you not know? Have you not heard?"

I don't understand it, & I can't explain it any better than this, but sometimes I just open my Bible & sob. As strange as the sensation is, I believe it is what I need to be doing until I don't feel compelled to do it anymore.

I had a moment just now where I didn't want to engage. I didn't want to talk to You, even *about* You to someone else. It always scares me.

It feels childish to compare myself to Jonah, who took that & ran & ran with it. Perhaps it is because of the otherworldly events in his life. Except being swallowed up by something all-encompassing can happen to me. It did happen to me. It is only childish to think it couldn't happen. It is only childish to think that healthy fear of God's peering eyes couldn't apply to me.

I do wonder about the mundane. It seems spineless, without form. But there is something to it. It is not the darkness God began with. It has shape, it has color God believes in creating. That makes the ordinary worth something. It makes me worth something.

All things new. All things new. All things new. That is a marvelous help. It is a rising of the never before living. New, new, new. To believe He cannot help me is the vapor, the thing that He will make into new belief stronger than the flesh I must rise from. I surrender.

As frustrating as it is to have so little control, it has never been about me. This story is much better than any anxious perfection, widespread, deliriously lacking in pain, any plan I could come up with on my own.

I always liked the Old Testament more. I understand it better. I understand the rules. I understand the wars better than I want to admit. Striking rocks with no reverence, loud mourning, loud violence, the slow years in judgement. I actually understand it better. I understand their exhaustion. I feel more comfortable with the order of animal sacrifice for my sins. It is terrifying how much it all adds up. The sense of order to it, however unfair, makes a kind of severed sense to me. The way it did to the Pharisees. *I can win this way. I can be good this way.*

Jesus as a child, the zooming in on everyday people, calming the waters instead of splitting them to the side, a verse explaining that Jesus was simply drawing in the sand. It's so much more quiet. It is so much more deafening. Jesus begged for water, & we gave Him vinegar as He was healing us. It makes my breathing jump. It makes me uncomfortable. There is nothing about it that makes sense. His blood over my sins means there is nothing I can do but accept a grace I do not deserve. I cannot offer Him anything He is happy to receive but my gratefulness.

The receiving of grace is accepting you do not understand it. It is what gives us access to the peace that doesn't make human sense either. You can do it, little heart. You take it. It is meant for you.

My inadequacies are painful to process. They are a lack of action & lack of experience. It's painful to look at that. God knows I feel that way, but He also knows He put me in this tension for a reason. To show me something. He controls where I am, who I am, so long as I turn myself over.

He gave me everything I have. If He is that powerful, He will show me what to do with all of it, even if He starts with me.

"For whenever our heart condemns us, God is greater than our heart, & He knows everything."

Do I rely on struggles to show my love for Him because I know I will need Him then? Is that why I am always struggling? What of a joyous season? I'm sure it will come when I stop believing it won't. Oh, little heart. He believes in you. He sees you.

There is a great anxiety when I start trying to collect all of the things I have secured for myself. *What have I done to keep people in my life? What did I do to secure my future? What did I secure for myself?*

Those questions begin & end with me. God doesn't think that way, so I must look up. *What will God secure for me? What did God already do?*

"For My own sake, for My own sake, I will do it."

Once I stop trying to push my way to the center of my own life & submit to God being there, I am overwhelmed by the new outlook I have. What looking up does to my questions. They become action oriented. There is no need to collect for myself because I begin to give.

How do I love today? What more can I do? How should I do it?

Some verses make me flinch when I read them. I am trying to see that any reading of the Bible, any taking in of what God says, is a good thing. It is the start.

The worst they can do is scare me away from who I am in Christ. I am strong in joy & capable in weakness & full of a terrified bravery to give up things that do not make me love the Christ that loves me. Who am I that I am afraid of man who dies?

What did the Lord say about it? What did God tell me to do? Have I spoken to Him about it?

I start feeling dirty, really very gross, from the things that I have seen, heard, & done. I think about Mark 7 every time. It is not what is outside of me that can hurt me, it is my response to it.

Turning away from things that make me feel hurt & pained is not always a type of hiding. Sometimes it's just smart. There is only one thing that can heal others, & it is not me.

When I'm Home, I remember God. I remember I do not have scars on my hands & sides. Dirty shameful feelings only come from trying to get relief from trying to be God all of the time. It's okay that I am not Him, He knows what I am. He made provisions for me.

There were moments of recoil between me & the church. It hurt, it was too bright, too suffocating. That's okay. Jeremiah felt that, Isaiah felt that, Jesus felt that. It comes & goes with the hurt. The church was still there afterwards, Jesus was still there, to welcome me back. It feels like an earthquake when relationships change, but shifted earth is not a permanent trip or disarming. In fact, once I adjusted, it revealed good. God does that so often.

"They know not what they do" was not a good enough reason for me to forgive them for many, many nights. It was incredibly humbling. I felt so much anger that I couldn't explain to anyone; those whom I tried to explain it to did not understand. They washed their hands clean of it before I had finished giving up any of my ghosts.

How did You do it? For a people who have to repent over & over? For us who only believe if we see? For me who cried out for so long at a God who had already shown me how to respond?

We sold Your clothes down at Your feet. We laughed at You. We killed Your ghost…we tried to kill Your ghost. Maybe that was a certain conciliation even on the cross, that You could already see our grateful faces in Heaven. That today You would be with the grateful little hearts in paradise.

The still moments after heaving emotion make it worth it. That feeling, it's almost a living thing, of God settling. Now I've made space for Him to do so in the midst of a trial He knew would cause more space in me. He knew I'd have to hand over so much to Him in order to keep going. Those tears, all those tears. My empty hands & all those tears.

A lot of times praying or coming to God with anything starts from scratch for me. I am alone with everything I always seem to bring to Him, bad parts of old days. I tell Him I struggle with thankfulness & understanding my worth. I tell Him I know He's done much for me. I tell Him how hard it is trying not to beat myself up for every little thing. I tell Him which verse is in my mind & why I think it's there. Then I get quiet, very quiet. Sometimes I feel Him there, sometimes I don't. On nights I don't, I wonder what the point was until I know for sure. The Lord just wanted to hear my voice speaking to Him.

Sometimes it's just a matter of doing what the Lord wants.

There is always a new thought to have about Christ & my story because it never ends. Oh, my little heart.

I do wonder who I would be if I remembered consistently that even in my pain, Jesus is working. Even in a desperate place, Jesus is doing something that no man can destroy, not even the one He is working in. It is Him, I cannot bind Him. I cannot stop His movement, His ability to change. Sometimes I want to, but I am always grateful I can't.

Do I need to see Him everywhere? Should I? Am I allowed to be exhausted? I suppose it's not a signal to stop entirely, only to rest. Rest is good. Rest after work is the only way to grow strong. I keep forgetting.

Joy from the Lord is from Himself. Joy from the world is dependent on other factors. I, for a time, believed I had consistent joy from Him with the certain blessings that stayed in my life. When they were taken away, I was immediately bold & embittered. *I thought I knew You,* I told Him. *I thought I could find You clearly in my life.*

It's as if I heard Him shake His head.

Think. What were you finding your strength in?

Oh, my little heart with little faith in it. The smallest mustard seed of hope in it. It will grow strong if He has anything to say about it. I'm glad He does.

The word "devour" is a big one for how small it is. I felt it so much.

I must not have been as devoured as I believed because I'm still here. None of my enemies nor the darkness of their dens, not even the lions inside them, destroyed me. Satan tries it all the time, it is a comfort & a healthy reminder that he never succeeds, even if it feels as if he has.

I have to start over all of the time. I have to re-evaluate often. I am learning to see even that differently, to believe it isn't a falling apart. It is an adding on to myself, not simply a breaking in me.

We are worth an incredible amount, the blood of Jesus. It puts my every other bias into perspective.

I keep the fact close that God does not ask for perfection. He asks for transparency. He asks me to set everything down to Him so that He can begin to fight for me. The cleansing of my soul, God uprooting sin from my life, is one of the most difficult but freeing experiences I know of.

Sometimes the voice of God sounds like that, like it could hurt me if I pressed into it harder. The Bible says it is the goodness of God that leads men to repentance.

His goodness. He will not harm me. & if there is pain, it is the kind that will make me stronger, like the soreness of muscles.

Singing gets hard. Joy gets hard. It's elusiveness in my life makes me think of the verse about God's singing over us & the many others about singing back to Him. If I look at joy like it's a conversation with God, experiences made up of Him, maybe it would open me up.

I'm afraid my prayers cheapen things. Devalue them. My heart feels like it's constantly shifting, it is not in a place to be aligned with what God wants.

It is me. It's that temple idea again. The fact that I am a vessel, considered sacred. There is nothing cheap about what God calls precious. Certainly not a voice that is trying to speak to Him.

They tore me limb from limb, & they aren't even sorry. They don't even want to take responsibility.

Jesus knows what that feels like. Jesus bore the physical wounds of such things. He forgave us as it was happening to Him.

Yes, but of course He did. He's God, & I'm not.

Exactly. But He still forgave.

I wonder if I'll ever think of a sentence big enough to grasp it. He bore our sorrows that were born out of the very actions that made Him bore our sorrows. He was crying out from the pain of our pain. The cross is a perfect example of that thing I can't find the right words for. This act of forgiveness while being in great anguish. Of being angry & loving. That middle ground. That tension of God turning away from Himself. It's that. It was in the flesh that was severed for me, & here I sit trying to dart away from it. I should step into it. God did because He knew it would give me the freedom to do so now.

They didn't tear me anymore than we tore You, & You forgave. I can forgive.

The Lord can handle my emotions, but He shouldn't have to. This is the guilt that eats me up if I let it. Yet there is never an ounce of God acting as if this is a difficult thing to take on. He created emotion itself. He is the embodiment of that just love so elusive to me. Of course He can take my feelings in. Of course He can. What's more is that He already has.

Satan will try to tell me that there is no point in praising because of my state of mind. That there is no way to get it out, certainly not by taking it to a perfect God. Yet this perfect God is my God. He receives anything I offer, then begins to mold it into something better. Always, always something better. Praising, getting my eyes off of myself, this is the point of my entire life.

It's His questions. It's always the questions He opens with. God's questions have always been that anxious standout in my mind's eye when I read them. I don't like how they sound. The question I want to ask back is the one I've been stumbling over most often. Why does my Father always sound so openly frustrated at them? At us? At me?

God's irreverence for pride when He asks, "Were you there when I laid the foundation of the earth?"
God's irreverence for shame when He asks, "What have you done?"
God's irreverence for lack of wisdom when He asks, "Did you eat from the tree?"

Jesus in the New Testament too. There are those frustrating & hard-to-explain quips from God in the flesh. "How long am I to be with you?"

I see it more now. It isn't that He is picking, or pushing, or wanting to hurt, but it's the sin in us. He hates it for us as much as He loves us. Now it sounds more like an exclamation, a banishment, a "get behind me, Satan!" in the form of a question. I find it to be a delicate balance that makes me dizzy when I try & capture it for myself. When I read those now, I will read them not to feel guilt, but to see what else He wants to separate from me.

Sometimes flashing thoughts look more like real pain. Since they are vivid, are they what I need to be focusing on? It isn't the real though. It is anxiety. It is okay that those two things are different. God is in both of those worlds with me.

There is just this constant idea of the Lord doing good or harm to someone in the Old Testament. Do this, & God will do that. Eye for an eye. I don't know how to reconcile all those pieces of the same God.

Job & David mention this idea that helps for me, though. They just press the Lord repeatedly with requests, with questions. By the time God answers, they are so silent. I think about that kind of quietness & can feel my heart stir.

"I thought on things too wonderful for me." & "Such knowledge is too wonderful for me; it is high; I cannot attain it."

God is everything we need. It's too much to wrap myself around. That's the point, I suppose. His thoughts are too high, His actions too wonderful. The word is romanticized, I think it's another word for powerful. It's the fearfulness of Him that gets stirred up in me next. He's so powerful it wouldn't matter unless He happened to care for me. & He does. There is His loving kindness & purposeful care.

They're right. It's a rather wonderful thing to see a glimpse of where all of our own sides come from. Even the trials we are subjected to are too wonderful to grasp.

I really like the idea of spirituality in everyday language. It doesn't have to mean something to others, just for me. It's that "but as for me" idea again.

I like saying "far be it from me" to people at work or saying in passing, "I'll be praying for you."

I think when I strive for church to meet my specific needs in its culture, so many of those "needs" get met when I begin to see God's idea of culture as something I can work on as an individual, that I can attain without others backing me up. Community starts with what I am willing to bring to the table as a believer. It can just be vulnerability & availability to start with. That's what community always starts with.

Humility comes from the Lord, & it feels healthy. There is gratefulness in it. Low self-esteem comes from pains & anger & insecurities. Frustrating that it's hard to differentiate, but it's getting easier all the time as I lift my eyes.

"Then whoever feared the word of the Lord hurried his slaves & his livestock into the houses, but whoever did not pay attention to the word of the Lord left his slaves & his livestock in the field."

It's just paying attention, just a matter of looking. The Lord wanted people believing. He wanted people of every background in the same house together. I spend so much time defending & working & pushing, even to myself, that I forget how much the word of God doesn't need any help being the truth that matters most.

I didn't think any dream could be bigger than the one I held previously. The dreams that have less health create such storms in my heart. It was a thrashing & wild monster that I was constantly trying to quiet, which felt like health but was just a coping. I couldn't figure out how to be grateful for it, & it always hurt me that I couldn't. I finally saw it in a flash as I looked down at my hands, which were always aching & empty.

It was letting it go. It was seeing it for the lack of goodness that it brought to me & how much bad it brought out of me.

The dream I held on to the tightest was the one I needed to let go of the most. It made so much room in me. My little heart had so much healing to do. All that room. *What was I to do with myself?*

I filled my heart up with You after that. You are so much bigger than anything I had carried previously.

Even if it wasn't what I thought it to be, I wonder why God allowed me to do something. Maybe there is something that is meant to happen there, even if it is just understanding that God is present no matter what is happening. I've had to grieve over that kind of thing before, something I prayed for but could not make work. I had to take time, move slowly, & to remember myself, my needs in a work space & in every other place in life. I know it's hard. I will be praying for all of the above because I want health.

Oh, little heart, I don't know where to go from here, but to Him.

But I want to be more. I want a clear mind & a willingness to improve, to face, & to serve. I know I am not receiving what You want me to, & it makes me want to run away. But I can't improve that way. I can't get to be where You want me that way. I am not enough, & I'll never be enough. Help me rest in my weakness, knowing You have me. That my weakness is not a bad thing.

God is here in my aching, aching bones.

Please use tomorrow for Your good. I know You will, You always do. I just wanted to submit that I don't want it to be used for anything else at all, if not for You.

It's okay to struggle, it's okay to ask. My Savior did. I press that truth close to myself so often because the Bible presses it so often.

Since the beginning, we start with no form, void, & darkness. God gifts us form, life, & light.

"Aaron & Hur held up his hands." What if Moses thought He could have done it alone? What if they decided they were not worthy to help Him? They all would have lost.

Do not feel like you need to fight by yourself in order to be good, little heart; you need help. Rejecting pride & embarrassment about weakness is where the fight begins.

Some get more than others. Are some better, special, closer to You? I don't think so. You are no respecter of persons. So what then? We are of small account, You know us & know what we need & want. You do what is best, what is perfect. Heaven is close, so close. Time is brief here. There is equal provision for all in Heaven. No matter our lot here, thank You for such things.

I hated reading Matthew 8 at first. I read it in glances because I hated that Jesus said, "Follow me, & leave the dead to bury their own dead."

Then I thought hard about the people I couldn't save. The people I followed to their graves of no belief. They didn't mean their actions towards me. Maybe I wouldn't hate Matthew 8 if I thought I would leave with Jesus instead of offering Him my lack of ability to save.

The interesting thing about our circumstances now, in which Jesus is not physically present, is that we have every single mental opportunity to turn & follow Him. There is no better time than now.

The dead, the people with bad fruit, they take care of themselves. They bury themselves. Sometimes, more times than not, it is just leaving them to *their* own devices & claiming what belongs to *me*. My own sin, my own life, my own bad fruit. Once I pick it up, & can hand it to Him. We all have things to shed. God knows.

It is in this very moment I understand it again. The grace of the Lord. That this understanding of the Lord's mercy uproots everything, even graves. Even my own. That I may have done that. I may have stayed too long in death, but I can go now to live, & He is glad I'm going.

Can it be believed that there is a reference to unintentional sin in the Old Testament? For something considered so archaic, God made so much room for growth during that time. I cannot know my mistakes while I make them. That's okay. I can make mistakes. He has made room for that. There is no damage He can't reverse if I am willing to admit there is something to fix. With Jesus's fulfillment of a law like that one, the grace is overwhelming.

For the first time in a long time, I feel rested & impartial to moments that I couldn't figure out how to heal from. It's a new kind of humming in my heart. It makes me take a deep breath as I write this, so full of gratefulness.

Sins others commit around you are not yours. So many times in the Bible, people point to others for refuge from guilt. So many times, I've done it. It is just before Jesus touches on what I am struggling with specifically. There is no room to point at anyone else. Even before repentance, Jesus is asking to heal me. I always am full of that guilt until I realize I remember why Jesus is asking to heal me in the first place. He knows me. He already knew.

God has told me things I never expected to get answers for. I have been given blessings I never imagined receiving. God has delivered me. God has changed me. I am only at the beginning.

I think a lot about Jesus in the desert & in the garden. He had allowed so much weakness to be shown to us. How unassuming He must have looked. His weight loss from fasting & tears in His eyes during prayers. God treated Him the way He treats us all. With steadfastness & fatherly support. Jesus wanted something, begged for something, but He did not get it. I think about it all the time. That His face sweat blood from veins underneath His skin, & God said He must endure more.

My God is split into three parts & in perfect harmony, there was action taken on my behalf while one part begged another other for relief. There is no shame in loving this God.

There is a fact that floats around me all the time, that if we are true to our word God will honor us with His.

What if I'm not true? I doubt it afterwards. *I feel like I'm never true.*

"Little heart," I can hear afterwards every time, "you are being true right now."

I got to a place where all the wells I knew of were poisoned. The very place I met Jesus was poisoned. I didn't know where to go after that. I didn't know where to find Jesus waiting for me. To help me. *Do I associate Jesus purely with those pains? Is it the only place He can meet me?*

I know this isn't true, even if I can still feel the past; it's the red aftertaste, that murk in my mouth. No. Jesus offers His own water. It is different than all the others. If I go to Him, even if I do not recognize the taste, I know as I drink it that it is only water with life. The only water. His water is a cleaning out of all old things. It is the only good thing. I can think it over some more, or I can drink & live.

The woman in the Bible left the well & even her water jar. The well & its dusty contents, where she met the Messiah, her first purpose for going there, it was all a means to an end. She left it all.

It is where she went afterwards, it is what she became as she left.

"Go." You said, "Go, & sin no more."

"Many Samaritans from that town believed in Him because of the woman's testimony."

John 4:39

Made in the
USA
Monee, IL